Festivals of the *World*

TURKEY

Gareth Stevens Publishing
MILWAUKEE

Written by
MARIA O'SHEA

Edited by
FIONA CONBOY

Designed by
JAILANI BASARI

Picture research by
SUSAN JANE MANUEL

First published in North America in 1999 by
Gareth Stevens Publishing
1555 North RiverCenter Drive, Suite 201
Milwaukee, Wisconsin 53212 USA

For a free color catalog describing Gareth
Stevens' list of high-quality books and multimedia
programs, call
1-800-542-2595 (USA)
or 1-800-461-9120 (Canada).
Gareth Stevens Publishing's Fax: (414) 225-0377.

© TIMES EDITIONS PTE LTD 1999
Originated and designed by
Times Books International
an imprint of Times Editions Pte Ltd
Times Centre, 1 New Industrial Road
Singapore 536196
Printed in Malaysia.

Library of Congress Cataloging-in-Publication Data:
O'Shea, Maria.
Turkey / by Maria O'Shea.
p. cm. — (Festivals of the world)
Includes bibliographical references and index.
Summary: Describes how the culture of Turkey
is reflected in its many festivals, including Seker
Bayrami, Kurban Bayrami, and the Kirkpinar
wrestling competition.
ISBN 0-8368-2037-1 (lib. bdg.)
1. Festivals—Turkey—Juvenile literature.
2. Turkey—Social life and customs—Juvenile literature.
[1. Festivals—Turkey. 2. Holidays—Turkey.
3. Turkey—Social life and customs.] I. Title. II. Series.
GT4873.5.A2074 1999
394.269561—dc21 99-14044

1 2 3 4 5 6 7 8 9 03 02 01 00 99

CONTENTS

It's Festival Time . . .

The Turkish word for festival is *bayram* (BAY-rahm). The most important festivals in Turkey are religious, but there are many cultural celebrations, too. Most Turkish *bayramli* (BAY-rahm-lee) revolve around foods—especially sweets—dancing, and singing. The bayram is a time for the people of Turkey to enjoy feasting and fancy dress with their families and friends. Join in the fun! It's festival time in Turkey . . .

WHERE'S TURKEY?

Turkey is a bridge between Europe and the Middle East and Asia. For over 600 years, this country was the heart of the massive Ottoman Empire that stretched across Europe, North Africa, and Arabia. Today, Turkey is a much smaller country. It became a **republic** in 1923. The capital city is Ankara, but the most famous city is Istanbul, which was once called Constantinople. Istanbul is the largest city in Turkey and the only city in the world to lie on two continents.

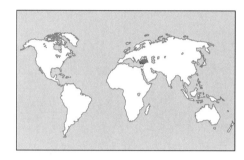

Who are the Turks?

Most Turkish people are Muslims, although there are small groups of Christians and Jews, too. The inhabitants of the Ottoman Empire were from many different countries and spoke many languages. Today, a group of people, called **Kurds**, who live in the eastern parts of Turkey, make up about one-fifth of the population, and the official language of the country is Turkish.

Turkish children often dress in national costume at festival time.

Opposite: Istanbul's Saint Sophia mosque was the largest enclosed space in the world for nearly 1,000 years.

TURKEY

BULGARIA

RUSSIA

GEORGIA

ARMENIA

IRAN

IRAQ

SYRIA

CYPRUS

GREECE

Black Sea

Sea of Marmara

Aegean Sea

Mediterranean Sea

Edirne
Istanbul
Marmara
Izmit
Iznik
Canakkale
Bursa
Eskisehir
Manisa
Izmir
Aydin
Marmaris
Fethiye
Antalya
Alanya
Silifke

Zonguldak
Sinop
Samsun

ANKARA
Bogazkale
Lake Tuz
Konya
Karaman Mts
Adana

Trabzon
Rize
Kars

Erzincan
Erzurum
Dogubeyazit
Divrigi
Elazig
Malatya
Van
Lake Van
Mt. Ararat
Diyarbakir
Gaziantep
Sanliurfa
Mardin

Kayseri

Kizil Irmak
Yesil Irmak
Pontic Mts
Sakarya
Gediz
Menderes
Taurus
Seyhan

N

WHEN'S THE BAYRAM?

Most people who live in Turkey are Muslims. Their calendar, called the **lunar calendar**, is based on the moon. It is 11 days shorter than the Western, or Gregorian, calendar, which is based on the sun. Consequently, religious festivals in Turkey fall on different days each year. Turkish people love celebrations, so, besides religious festivals, they have lots of national and local festivals throughout the year, too.

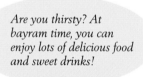

Are you thirsty? At bayram time, you can enjoy lots of delicious food and sweet drinks!

RELIGIOUS FESTIVALS

- ✪ **SEKER BAYRAMI**
- ✪ **KURBAN BAYRAMI (THE FEAST OF THE SACRIFICE)**
- ✪ **MEVLID-I NEBI (THE PROPHET'S BIRTHDAY)**—People read poems about the birth of the Prophet Mohammed and cook special sweet dishes, and the children exchange colored eggs.
- ✪ **THE MEVLANA FESTIVAL**—Whirling Dervishes perform to honor a great poet who founded the Jalaladin Rumi religious order.

NATIONAL FESTIVALS

- ✪ **CUCUK BAYRAMI**
- ✪ **YOUTH AND SPORTS DAY**
- ✪ **CUMHURIYET BAYRAMI**—All towns in Turkey have parades and speeches to commemorate the proclamation of the Turkish Republic in 1923.
- ✪ **VICTORY DAY**—This day celebrates Turkey's victory over invading Greek forces in the War of Independence in 1922.

Read all about the dance of the Whirling Dervishes on page 13.

SEASONAL FESTIVALS

- ✪ **NEW YEAR'S DAY**
- ✪ **KIRKPINAR WRESTLING**—In the biggest wrestling competition in Turkey, competitors cover themselves with oil and wrestle wearing only knee-length calfskin pants.
- ✪ **ST. NICHOLAS FESTIVAL**—Celebrations are held in the old church of St. Nicholas, the original Santa Claus, in southern Turkey.
- ✪ **KURDISH NEW YEAR**—Although not an official holiday, the large Kurdish population celebrates the new year on March 21st.

SEKER BAYRAMI

The festival of Seker Bayrami (she-KER BAY-rahm-ee) is described by the Turkish expression "sweet food, sweet talk." This festival is known to other Muslims by its Arabic name, Eid el-Fitr (eed el-FIT-ter). It follows a month of fasting called **Ramazan**. Seker Bayrami has become associated with delicious sweet foods and children's entertainments.

What a relief!

During the month of Ramazan, Muslims all over the world are forbidden to eat or drink from sunrise to sunset. In Turkey, the last night of Ramazan ends with a special feast of all the family's favorite foods. This feast is the beginning of the Seker Bayrami festival.

Early the next morning, everyone rises to wash and put on their new clothes. Because cutting hair during Ramazan is forbidden, barber shops are very busy. People also cut their nails for the first time in a month. Muslims visit the mosque in the morning to pray, giving thanks that Ramazan was successfully completed with God's help. Women may pray at home while they are busily preparing lunch for their guests.

Young children do not have to fast during Ramazan, but they try to fast as soon as they are old enough.

Above: This sacred pool is a
gathering place for Turkish Muslims
during Seker Bayrami.

Exchanging gifts

Throughout the festival of Seker Bayrami, Turkish people
exchange gifts and cards, which they bought during Ramazan.
As a special treat, children receive new clothes and toys.

The poor are not forgotten either—each family leaves a
special gift of money for them. The price of one meal for
each family member, including any unborn children, is
given at the mosque to be distributed to the needy in
Turkey or abroad. Some generous people donate
much larger sums.

The Ramazan fast requires great
discipline. Muslims pray for
God's help during this time.

Visiting family and friends

Seker Bayrami is a special time for family and friends. People rush to visit one another to celebrate together. Older people become angry if they think they have not been visited promptly. Close family members sometimes give each other gifts. Children, however, expect to receive money from all the adults to whom they offer wishes for a happy bayram. It is no wonder that children are eager to visit as many houses as possible! They learn to greet adults in a special way. They bow and kiss the adult's hand, then touch their own foreheads to show love and respect. If they cannot visit an older relative, they must telephone the person and say they would like to kiss his or her hand.

In small Turkish towns and villages, Seker Bayrami is still celebrated in very traditional ways, with the elders of the town singing and dancing to traditional Turkish music and with wrestling competitions. Wrestling is one of the most popular sports in Turkey.

It is important for the whole family to enjoy the Seker Bayrami celebrations together.

Above: Turkish Delight is a candy made from sugar and gelatin.

Sweet surprises

Some foods are associated with special Turkish events, such as a religious festival, a child's first day at school, or a wedding. Whatever the occasion, everyone in the family helps prepare the festival food.

In all Turkish houses, guests are offered tea, coffee, and rich sweets on Seker Bayrami. The sweets may be wrapped in pretty handkerchiefs when distributed to guests. Trays of specially wrapped bayram sweets are both offered in homes and taken to the neighbors. Many women stay up all night preparing these special sweets, cakes, pastries, and puddings.

Turkish towns decorate the streets with fairy lights for the bayram. In some places, fun fairs and amusement parks are set up for families to enjoy.

Turkey is famous for its desserts and sweets. Seker Bayrami is a time for everyone to enjoy the delights of Turkish cuisine.

Think about this

Looking forward to Seker Bayrami is one way Turkish Muslims get through the Ramazan fast. Sometimes, parents promise their children special gifts if they can manage the fast, even for just a day. Imagine how you would feel eating a meal at midday for the first time in a month!

Festivals of Dance

Dancing is an important part of Turkish festivals, and each region has its own special dance. There are over 1,500 different types of Turkish folk dances in existence. Asian tribes **devised** these folk dances hundreds of years ago, and their passionate and energetic movements are still enjoyed today.

The city of Konya is the center of Sufism in the Middle East today.

Communication through dance

A poet, named Jalaladin Rumi, developed a religion called Sufism in the 13th century. Sufism kept the basic principles of **Islam**, but included a dramatic change—the addition of music and dance as ways to communicate with God. Islam forbids dancing.

Dancing for the love of God

The Whirling Dervishes follow Sufism, and every year, in December, visitors to the city of Konya watch them communicate with God through movement. The music of an instrument called the *nay* represents God's voice in the dance. The dancers accompany the music with a rhythmic chant and whirl for hours in a trancelike state. Both tourists and Turks flock to Konya to see these dancers in their distinctive robes at the Mevlana Festival.

The Whirling Dervishes wear white robes that flare out as they dance. Their conical hats are made from camel's hair.

Turkish dancers often wear costumes that include all the colors of the rainbow. This girl is performing the spoon dance.

Think about this
Turkish people love to dance! The biggest outdoor discotheque in Europe is on Turkey's Aegean coast. Also, Turkey is famous for the belly dance, which actually originated in Spain. Can you think of any music or dance styles that your country is famous for?

Folk festivals

Turkish villages were cut off from the rest of the world for hundreds of years. As a result, each one developed its own folk festivals and dances, so there is no one typical Turkish folk dance. Most of the dances are performed by groups. Originally, they celebrated the birth of a child, a young couple's marriage, or the return of men from military service. Every folk festival held in Turkey provides great insight into its history and village life.

Traditional dances

A traditional Turkish folk dance, called the spoon dance, is best known in the area around the town of Silifke on the Mediterranean coast. Spoon dancers wear vivid costumes and make dance rhythms with wooden spoons, clicking them together like **castanets**.

The sword and shield dance of Bursa is performed to commemorate the conquest of that town by the Ottoman forces. These dancers wear warriorlike costumes.

Black Sea Festival

The Black Sea Festival celebrates the traditions of people living in the Black Sea region. It stems from the worship of Cybele, the goddess of fertility. It is said that Cybele wore a special stone in her crown, so, at these festivals today, women throw pebbles into the sea, hoping that the ritual will bring them children. Local men dress in black and silver costumes to perform a dance called the Horon.

Horon dancers at the Black Sea Festival join hands as they move to the vibrating rhythms of the music.

Right: Folk festival music tells a story. This instrument, called a *saz*, accompanies singing storytellers.

15

KURBAN BAYRAMI

The Feast of the Sacrifice, or Kurban Bayrami [KOOR-bon BAY-rahm-ee], is one of the most important Islamic festivals. It celebrates a special religious event—the Prophet Abraham's willingness to do whatever God asked of him. Muslims living in other parts of the world call this festival by its Arabic name, Eid el-Adha [eed el-AHD-ha].

On this day, Turkish cities and towns are filled with animals to be sacrificed. Traditionally, the animals are decorated with **henna**.

Above: For days before the festival, shepherds from all parts of Turkey travel to towns with their flocks.

Villagers with Turkish flags lead a procession at the annual Kurban Bayrami parade.

Listen to a story

Ibrahim (the Muslim name for Abraham) was a very special man—he was a prophet of God. He had two sons, Ismail and Ishak, who were believed to be miraculous rewards from God for Ibrahim's service to him. God tested the strength of Ibrahim's love, however, with a terrifying request.

God ordered Ibrahim to make a fire and offer his son, Ismail, as a **sacrifice**. Ibrahim was devastated, but Ismail agreed that they must carry out God's wishes. Ibrahim took Ismail to the sacrifice altar, but, as he was about to strike Ismail, God held back Ibrahim's hand and sent an animal for the sacrifice, instead. Ismail was saved, and Ibrahim had proven his love for God.

Families gather to select an animal for the bayram sacrifice. Everyone wants to buy the healthiest, plumpest sheep in town.

Whole sheep are roasted on spits after the sacrifice. A roasting spit is like an old-fashioned barbecue!

Making a sacrifice

Kurban Bayrami celebrates Ibrahim's and Ismail's willingness to make the sacrifice God requested of them. On this day, all Muslims try to make a sacrifice, usually a sheep. Then they give at least a third of the meat to the poor and a third to their families and friends. A very **generous** Muslim will buy an animal for a poor family to sacrifice, so that family can share in the celebration, too.

The sacrifice is offered in the accepted Islamic way. The animal must be in good health, well-fed, and not thirsty, so it is always offered water before the sacrifice. Its throat is slit in one movement, and the blood is allowed to drain away completely, making the meat *halal* [hal-ARL], or safe, for Muslims to eat.

The wool from sheep sacrificed on Kurban Bayrami is often spun and woven into a rug. The rug is considered lucky.

A big feast

In the morning of Kurban Bayrami, Muslims visit the mosque to offer a special prayer to God. Everyone wears clean or new clothes and visits family and friends. Children kiss the hands of adults to get money or sweets from them, and adults kiss the hands of those older than themselves.

In addition to all the sweets, fruits, and drinks, there is a big feast prepared using the sacrificed meat. Families often send samples of their cooked meat dishes to other houses, and everyone eats a lot, even the poor, who can count on having donated meat. Invited guests either arrive with trays of fresh meat from their sacrifices or send offerings. The streets are filled with stalls selling **kebabs** and other meat dishes.

Kurban Bayrami is the longest festival period in Turkey, so many people like to take a holiday trip. The few days before this festival are the busiest days of the year to travel in Turkey.

Think about this

There are over 50 million sheep in Turkey—which is nearly as many sheep as people! Some people, especially in the countryside, treat these animals like pets. Facing the responsibility of sacrificing the animals makes Muslims realize how hard it must have been for Ibrahim to pass God's test, thinking that he had to sacrifice his son. To kill an animal with little suffering is an important Muslim duty.

Street stalls selling kebabs and tasty meat snacks are always busy on Kurban Bayrami!

Children's Festivals

I
n 1923, Mustafa Kemal was elected the first president of Turkey. He modernized the country, and it became part of Europe. He gave every adult the right to vote for a parliament and declared that all Turks should choose a last name. Kemal took the name *Ataturk*, which means "father of the Turks."

Right: Mustafa Kemal Ataturk was Turkey's first president.

Ataturk's children

At the time Ataturk came to power, nine out of ten Turkish people couldn't read or write. Ataturk saw the future of Turkey in its children and declared that all children must attend school and learn to read and write. He built many schools and insisted that all students wear black uniforms, so it was not clear who was rich and who was poor.

Ataturk loved the children of Turkey so much that he established an annual holiday just for them. He called the holiday Cucuk Bayrami.

Cucuk Bayrami gives Turkish children time to have fun with their friends!

A holiday for the children

On Cucuk Bayrami, children all over Turkey dress in national costumes or fancy dress and perform plays. The main event on this special day takes place in Ankara, Turkey's capital city, where children from around the world take part in a spectacular display of singing and dancing.

Every school organizes a play or a musical, and children can show their own special abilities in music, singing, dancing, and acting. On Saturdays before the bayram, Turkish children often attend folklore classes, where they learn traditional dances and songs and how to play traditional Turkish instruments. Children often dress in the special costumes of the regions from which they have learned a dance when they perform in front of audiences at the bayram celebrations.

In many towns, the main event of Cucuk Bayrami is held in the sports stadium. Children from countries all over the world are invited to demonstrate their traditions, dances, and songs. The areas around the stadium are packed with stalls selling favorite snacks and foods. Inside the stadium, the stage is filled with colorful displays of music and dance.

Children spend hours rehearsing their performances and making their special festival costumes.

Youth and Sports Day

Ataturk was responsible for deposing the last **sultan** of the Ottoman Empire in 1923. He became known as the father of modern Turkey, having made dramatic **reforms** to the country during his rule. A special day on the Turkish calendar allows the young people of Turkey to celebrate the birthday of Mustafa Kemal Ataturk, the founder of the Turkish Republic, with sporting events and parades. This special day, called Youth and Sports Day, is held in May each year.

Turkish folk dresses are made with beautiful, brightly colored cloth, embroidered with flowers, and decorated with gold accessories.

Sporting competitions

On Youth and Sports Day, the children of Turkey celebrate with sporting events, such as soccer, wrestling, or javelin throwing. They enjoy dressing in national costume and putting on a great show!

Above and *below:* The shows at Youth and Sports Day celebrations are lots of fun! Some of the costumes are very unusual, too!

Think about this

Children's festivals help the young people of Turkey learn about the different ways people live in their country. Classes are held to teach children the dances of distant regions, rather than just their own. Ataturk wanted to show children that Turkey was one country, despite its large size and many cultures.

23

KIRKPINAR WRESTLING

In 1360, 40 warriors were invited to wrestle to honor the sultan and for the glory of God. Two finalists wrestled long into the night. At dawn, some spectators returned to find a terrible sight. The two wrestlers were still on their feet in the dusty field, but they had died of exhaustion. When they were removed from the field, 40 springs of clear water appeared, turning the dusty field into a lush green meadow. The place was called *Kirkpinar*, which means "Forty Springs."

The area became famous, and, for the last 60 years, an annual three-day festival has been held in Edirne in July.

Before the contest begins, a referee, or umpire, distributes watered-down olive oil to all the competitors.

The wrestlers

There are usually about 1,000 wrestlers competing at Kirkpinar in search of fame, glory, and cash prizes. All the wrestlers wear calfskin pants and cover themselves with watered-down olive oil, so their opponents cannot get a good grip on them.

The main contest

The classes in the competition are measured by height, not weight. The hero class is for the tallest 40 contestants. Colorfully dressed referees watch for illegal moves and declare the wrestler whose opponent falls exhausted the winner. The matches last between half an hour and three hours. After a victory, the wrestlers pair off, again and again, until only one is left standing. The winner is awarded the famous golden belt of Kirkpinar.

The olive oil is watered down so the wrestlers' skin doesn't burn under the hot sun.

THINGS FOR YOU TO DO

Many Turkish families are large, so, after school, the children have a lot of chores to do at home, on the farm, or in the family business. Festivals offer a break from this routine, and all children look forward to the special foods and entertainments that a festival will bring! Poorer children may eat sweets or have a day's rest from work only on festival days. Then they excitedly join their friends in a day or more of play and visiting each other's houses. Of course, farm work never stops, even for a day, but festivals mean fun anyway!

Play a game with five pebbles

This is the kind of game Turkish children play outside on bayram days, when they don't go to school.

1. Find five small pebbles. Throw them all into the air at the same time, and let them fall to the ground.

2. Pick up one of the five pebbles and throw it into the air. As it is falling, pick up a pebble from the ground, then catch the falling pebble in the same hand.

3. Put one of the pebbles aside and repeat step 2, picking up the other three pebbles in exactly the same way.

4. Start again, this time picking up two pebbles from the ground after you have thrown a pebble into the air. The next time, pick up three pebbles and, finally, pick up all four pebbles on the ground in one sweep while the fifth is in the air.

RAKKAS

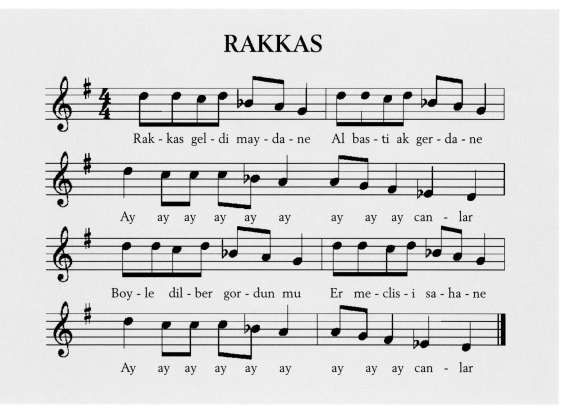

Rak - kas gel - di may - da - ne   Al bas - ti ak ger - da - ne

Ay ay ay ay ay ay   ay ay ay can - lar

Boy - le dil - ber gor - dun mu   Er me - clis - i sa - ha - ne

Ay ay ay ay ay ay   ay ay ay can - lar

The dancer

There is always lots of singing and dancing at Turkish festivals. This song, called *Rakkas*, in Turkish, is sung at the Black Sea Festival.

The dancer took to the stage, a sigh escaped our hearts,
Oh oh oh dear friends,
Have you ever set eyes upon such grace, oh happy gathering,
Oh oh oh dear friends.

Things to look for in your library

Eat Smart in Turkey: How to Decipher the Menu, Know the Market Foods and Embark on a Tasting Adventure. Joan Peterson (Gingko Press, 1996).
Mystery of the Kaifeng Scroll: A Vivi Hartman Adventure. Harriet K. Feder (Lerner Publications Company, 1995).
Travel Turkey: Turkish Coasts and Istanbul. (Victory Audio Video, 1994).
A Treasury of Turkish Folktales for Children. Barbara K. Walker (Linnet Books, 1997).
Turkey. (http://www.smm.org/catal, 1998).
Turkey. Cultures of the World (series). Sean Sheehan (Times Books International, 1996).

MAKE A TURKISH KILIM

The women of Turkey weave *kilims* (ki-LEEMs), or rugs and carpets, for their homes and to sell. Kilims are made to hang on the walls, cover drafty doors, sit on and sleep on, as well as put on the floor. The designs are mostly geometric, which means they are patterned with square, triangular, and rectangular shapes.

You will need:
1. Cardboard, 6" x 8" (15 x 20 cm)
2. 2 balls of yarn in red and orange or other bright colors
3. Scissors
4. Pencil
5. Ruler

2

5

1

4

3

1 Cut 1-inch (2.5-cm) slits into the top and bottom corners of the cardboard, 1 inch (2.5 cm) from the sides.

2 Make a knot at the end of the orange yarn and insert it in the top left-hand slit. Pull the yarn down and insert it in the bottom left-hand slit. Wrap the yarn tightly around the cardboard and knot it in place at the right-hand side.

3 Weave the red yarn over and under the orange yarn and tie it to the orange yarn. Continue weaving until the cardboard is covered.

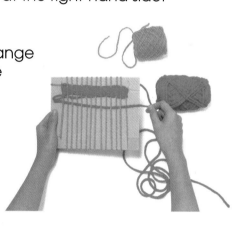

4 When you're finished weaving, cut the 2 middle orange threads at the back in the center and tie the threads together at each side. Continue cutting and tying orange threads to the left and right of the 2 middle threads.

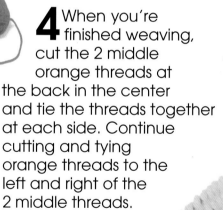

5 When you have tied all the orange threads, take the weaving off the cardboard. Cut the side strings evenly to make fringe. Now you have a colorful Turkish kilim!

MAKE A PUMPKIN DESSERT

T he Turks love to eat sweets and desserts — and not only at festival time. Pumpkins are popular in Turkey. They are sold at markets and shops and can be used in both sweet and spicy recipes. This pumpkin dessert is very easy to make and is a healthy alternative to the rich, sweet *baklava* (BAH-klah-vah) pastries found on the menus of most Turkish restaurants.

You will need:
1. ½ sweet pumpkin, washed and sliced into wedges
2. 1½ cups (150 grams) granulated sugar
3. ½ cup (50 g) walnuts
4. Spoon
5. Wide saucepan
6. Measuring cup

1 Place the pumpkin wedges over the bottom of the saucepan. Ask an adult to put the pan carefully on a hot stove.

2 Spoon the sugar over the pumpkin wedges and pour enough water into the pan to cover the pumpkin pieces. Cover the pan and cook over medium heat until the pumpkin is tender.

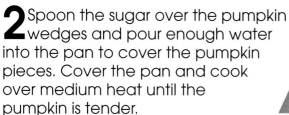

3 Ask an adult to help you put the pumpkin wedges on a dish. Sprinkle the wedges with chopped walnuts and allow them to cool. Eat this sweet treat with a knife and fork.

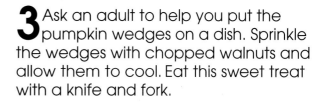

GLOSSARY

castanets, 14	Instruments made of two pieces of wood that are fastened to the thumb and clicked together with the other fingers.
devised, 12	Formed an idea or a plan in the mind.
generous, 18	Having a sharing and giving spirit, not mean or stingy.
henna, 16	A reddish-brown dye that comes from a tropical plant.
Islam, 12	The Muslim religion.
kebabs, 19	Roasted or grilled meat served in bread or on a skewer.
Kurds, 4	An ethnic group living in eastern Turkey.
lunar calendar, 6	A calendar based on the phases of the moon.
Ramazan, 8	The Muslim month of fasting and prayer, known as Ramadan in other Muslim countries.
reforms, 22	Changes or improvements.
republic, 4	A country run by its government, not by a King or a Queen.
sacrifice, 17	An act of offering to a god.
sultan, 22	A kinglike leader, or ruler, of a land, usually Muslim.

INDEX

Picture credits
ANA Press Agency: 7 (bottom); Andes Press Agency: 9 (top), 10, 11 (right), 13; Michele Burgess: 12, 14; Camera Press: 21; Gladys Chee: 17; Focus Team: 3 (top); Hans Hayden: 6, 9 (bottom); B. Klingwall: 15 (bottom), 19, 28; Robert Leon: 7 (top); Photobank: 3 (bottom), 5; Travel Ink: 18 (bottom); Trip: 2, 4, 11 (left), 16 (both), 18 (top), 20 (left), 22, 24; Turkish Ministry of Tourism: 1, 8, 15 (top), 20 (right), 23 (both), 25

Digital scanning by
Superskill Graphics Pte Ltd.